LOOK AT THE BIRDS

ANGELA MCCAULEY

To Pat

LOOK AT THE BIRDS

Angela McCauley

For my parents John & Winifred McEvoy

LEISURE

What is this life if full of care
We have no time to stand and stare
No time to stand beneath the boughs
And stare as long as sheep and cows
No time to see when woods we pass
Where squirrels hide their nuts in grass
No time to see in broad daylight
Streams full of stairs like skies at night
No time to turn at beauty's glance
And watch her feet how they dance
No time to wait till her mouth can
Enrich that smile her eyes began
A poor life this is full of care
We have no time to stand and stare.

By W H Davies

INTRODUCTION

O ur fourteen birds have flown the nest. We have eight boys and six girls. Most are married and some are living in the nations. All have at least one degree from a top UK University. When it was time for my husband Brendan and I to leave our empty nest in Saul Street, Downpatrick we downsized to a bigger house on the shores of Strangford Lough in Portaferry.

The sea was at the bottom of our garden. We could watch the sun rise and the ferry crossing from our large kitchen window. Our home in Downpatrick had seven bedrooms, a shower room, a bathroom and three toilets. Our new house had six bedrooms, two of them ensuite, two ordinary bathrooms and two toilets.

It was a dream home or rather it was my husband's dream house. Brendan actually dreamed about this large beautiful house a year earlier.

We lived in this home for six years and our children

and grandchildren came and holidayed, picnicked, swam and boated in the sea at the bottom of our garden.

Four years earlier God had healed me of fourth stage colon cancer and Brendan wrote a book about it called, *Staying Alive!* He also wrote about our early life of faith called, *The Grapes Are Worth It!*

I believe God brought us to beautiful Portaferry in order to heal me from the trauma leading to having cancer. The nine centimetre cancerous tumour as big as an orange had disappeared. It's one thing to be cured from a life threatening cancer. It's another thing to be healed from the ordeal.

I needed to be healed from the disappointments and despair I felt at life not working out the way I wanted. My children had grown up, left home, and were doing well in studies, work and life. I was missing them. Our success at rearing our children gave them the strength to face life and succeed. But I felt they didn't need me any more. I had to let all my ideas go and trust God to show His plan for my future.

I have listened to prophetic words about God using me in healing. That hope wasn't working out either. Here I was needing healing myself. A hope fulfilled is a tree of life but a hope deferred makes the heart sick. [1]

In 1991 the neurocardiologist Dr Armour discovered the heart has its own 'little brain' composed of 40,000 neurons that are similar to the neurons in our brains. This means our hearts have a brain and a memory. My heart's memory needed healing.

We can all suffer from stress and anxiety. We worry. Worrying will not change what happens. Jesus instructed his disciples. He said,

> I tell you do not worry about your life, what you will eat or drink; or about your body what you will wear. Is not life more than food and the body more than clothes? Look at the birds of the air they do not sow nor reap or store into barns and yet your Heavenly Father feeds them. Are you not more valuable than they? Can any one of you by worrying add a single hour to your life? Your Heavenly Father knows you have need of them. But seek first the Kingdom of God and all these things will be given to you as well[2]

Watching the birds of the air has healed my mind and taught me to trust God. I have quieted myself to look at creation all around and learned to cast my care upon the Lord and not worry.

Strangford Lough is one of the most important areas for birds in all of Ireland. At peak times it is home to more than 20,000 waterfowl and over 40,000 waders. It's a bird-watchers paradise. In our home in Ballyhenry House I did what Jesus recommended. I became a birdwatcher.

This book is a collection of blogs and poems about the

many birds that lived in my garden, in the nearby forest and the sea birds that came to live on Strangford Lough.

During our six years in Ballyhenry House, Loughshore Road, Portaferry, Brendan and I hosted family and friends, gatherings and visitors from the nations. We also travelled, ministered and wrote books.

But best of all we also walked and explored the teeming shoreline and trekked the nearby Nugent's Wood especially when it was carpeted in a million swaying bluebells.

Portaferry was a place of healing for us. The sun and the moon shine brightly there. When the sun went down after a bright day the sky became a vista of pale orange, yellow, grey and blue outlining the hills and valleys of Co Down.

This book is a story of my healing of mind and heart as I looked at the birds and creation all around me. I quote from the scriptures because I love the Bible. These are words that were relevant to my every day life in Portaferry.

> The moon will be as bright as the sun, and
> the sun will be seven times brighter—like
> the light of seven days in one! So it will
> be when the Lord begins to heal his
> people.[3]

RESTORATION

$\mathcal{I}$ was born in Newcastle, Co Down. My parents moved to a farm near Ballynahinch when I was one year old, the youngest of six children, one son and five girls. It was a time of change for mum and dad as they prepared to raise their family in a new area. Dad was a visionary and a man of faith. He moved to Dunmore, Co. Down. It was near a girl's grammar school in Ballynahinch. He wanted his girls to get educated.

If a father or mother is a doctor some of their children are doctors. If parents are musical their children will be musical. I met a lady who was the daughter of three generations of preachers. My mother had ten children, her mother had fifteen children. I took after my mother. I grew up with my family where mum and dad laid down their lives to care for us. It was after I had children of my own and the struggles that brings that I appreciated my parent's sacrifice. I went to university in Coleraine when I was eighteen years old. I lived there, got married, finished university, grew in faith, and reared our fourteen children.

Our home in Coleraine soon became too small for our growing family. I knew our children would need more space as they became teenagers. I began to pray that God would lead us to a bigger home. Where could we move to? I didn't know but I did believe God would have somewhere.

After the ceasefire in 1998 we moved to Co Down. I returned to where I grew up. God gave me this promise some years before. "I will restore you to your father's land and I will heal you." God also gave this promise to the Jewish people and now they are returning to live in the land of Israel.[1]

We lived for a year in Ballynahinch in the same street my mother and father had lived in after they retired from the farm. Sadly my parents were not alive to see my return. I felt I returned to my tribe. God brought me back to my father's land.

While in Ballynahinch, Brendan was reading Seamus Heaney's book *Wintering Out*. We felt our stay in Ballynahinch would be a short one, just over the winter. This proved to be the case. It was enough time to rest after our move from Coleraine.

Our family adjusted after the move from Coleraine. We had been through a few months of upheaval from the security of our home in Coleraine. I believed God was answering my prayers to bring us to a bigger home, my promised land, to rear our still growing family. Just as my father had done.

Brendan continued family routines of bedtime prayers and times out for walks in forests or beaches. We maintained stability in the midst of change. Changes for the better.

Near where we lived there was a corn mill, where I remembered going with my father to get grain milled. The water from the river at the back of our house fed the corn mill's grinding wheel. The mill had fallen into disrepair.

My son John met new friends in Ballynahinch. He spent his weekends with them discovering our new locality. His adventures reminded me of the poem, *Keepsake Mill*, by Robert Louis Stevenson.

Over the borders, a sin without pardon,
Breaking the branches and crawling below
Out through the breaching he wall of then
    garden
Down to the banks of the river we go.

Here is the mill with the humming of
    thunder
Here is the weir with the wonder of foam
Here is the sluice with the race running
    under
Marvellous places though handy to home.

. . .

Our children, Patrick, David, Jacob, Isaac and Abraham attended St Patrick's Primary School in Ballynahinch. Four of their cousins attended the same school. Our daughter Ruth attended Assumption Grammar, the same school I went to. It was good for my young children to see where I grew up and meet uncles and aunts and relatives who lived nearby.

Aunty Kathleen lived in the same street. I was able to call in for coffee often. Our new neighbours welcomed us with open arms to their Halloween party when we arrived at our new home. It was as if we'd always lived there.

The year 2000 was Brendan's fiftieth year. It was a year of Jubilee, new beginnings. My sister Eileen, who lived in Washington, USA suggested we have a family reunion of all our ten families. My sisters Maureen, Una, Kathleen, Rosaleen, Carol and Deirdre and brothers Patsy and Gerard arranged a celebration at Gerard's home place.

Eileen returned from the USA with her family. We all gathered and attended Mass for thanksgiving. At Gerard's we had a barbecue, drinks, games, sports, and party pieces. It was a memorable and fun day for all of us. My children got to see many relatives in our extended family they'd never met before. It helped their sense of identity and belonging.

The following year was my year of Jubilee. I celebrated my fiftieth birthday. We moved to Downpatrick to rent a

seven bedroom house large enough for our big family. I
read about Moses.

> Divide the land among the tribes in propor-
> tion to their population. Give the larger
> tribes more land and the smaller tribes
> less land.[2]

God gave me a home according to the size of my tribe.
Some people think Brendan and I were crazy to have
fourteen children. Brendan said he was crazy - crazy
for me!

People asked questions such as, How are you going to
feed all your children? How can you afford to pay all the
bills? Where will you get a home big enough for your
family? Why are your children not sick? Your children
will not get enough attention. Do your children sleep at
night?

While in Ballynahinch I watched a nature programme
about the wild life in the North of India. The Brahma-
putra river flows through a wide area of the land. All
plants and wildlife flourish there. Some of the largest
animals in the world live together, the wild oxen,
elephants and tigers.

The programme showed a clip of a family of otters
lying in the sun on the bank of the river, each one
chewing on fresh fish. There is plenty of provision for
them all. I thought of my own family. God was reas-

suring me that as he looks after the wild animals so he will care for our family.

Brendan and I believe God wanted us to have all our children. They are all accepted and loved. We believed God's Word to seek first the Kingdom of God. God has been faithful to care for all of us and provide all our needs. We cast all our care upon The Lord.

LOOK FOR THE ANCIENT PATHWAYS

*W*hile war was going on in Northern Ireland, many people were seeking peace. They prayed to Jesus, the Prince of Peace[1]. It was a shame the trouble in Northern Ireland was over religion.

In Coleraine where we lived, some people who believed in Jesus, Catholics, Church of Ireland, Pentecostal, Baptist and Presbyterian, met together to pray for peace. God blesses unity.

> How good and pleasant it is when brothers
>   dwell in unity. [2]

I joined a group of ladies from different backgrounds who prayed. We met every week. I continued to pray with others while living in Coleraine. We lived and reared our children in this atmosphere of peace in Coleraine for twenty three years.

It is a big job rearing a big family. Brendan and I certainly wanted to be able to do the work with the least stress. We lived in Captain Street. Our younger children walked to school at St John's Primary. The boys went to Coleraine Institute. The older girls attended Loreto Grammar and The Girls Green High. I could walk to the shops, post office, doctor's surgery, dentist, library, takeaways and swimming pool. Everything was very near.

The home we lived in was adequate for our young children. I knew they would need more space as they became teenagers. After five years God led us to live in Co Down. When I told teachers and friends we were moving they said you will never get good schools like we have in Coleraine. Everything is convenient here. Why are you leaving? Your children will never settle. They thought we were crazy. But I believed God had a bigger home and brighter future for us.

The Word of God in Jeremiah says to look for the ancient pathways to find rest for our souls.

> "This is what the Lord says: Stop at the crossroads and look around. Ask for the old, godly way, and walk in it. Travel its path, and you will find rest for your souls". [3]

In 2000 we found a big house for our nine remaining children in Downpatrick, Co Down. Brendan had a dream that led us to connect with a Christian man called John

Thompson. John and his wife Linda helped us with the house.

The leaders of the different churches in the Downpatrick met together every month and prayed; ministers from the Catholic Church, Presbyterian Church, Churches of Ireland, Baptist, and the Unitarian Church met together. On Good Friday each year Christians walked the streets of Downpatrick and carried a cross and prayed.

We joined a Downpatrick Christian Fellowship. They prayed for our family. We will be ever grateful for their kindness and generosity. Downpatrick has an atmosphere of peace like Coleraine. I joined a women's prayer group in Downpatrick. We prayed for one another as we reared our children.

There were schools and clubs suitable for our growing teenagers. Hannah and John attended St Patrick's Grammar, a Catholic school. Hannah was made head girl. John was made head boy a few years later. Our children were well received. This was completely different from our daughter Mary's experience in the Protestant school she attended in Coleraine. She was a clever pupil but she was denied a prefect position in her last year, while every other girl in her year was given a prefect position. We received favour in Downpatrick. It is along an ancient pathway. St Patrick worked around this area in the sixth century. He is buried here. I was healed from fourth stage cancer while living in Downpatrick. Many people praying for me brought about my healing. Jesus heals today.

The tourist board of Northern Ireland has mapped out the St Patrick's trail which helps visitors travel to areas where early Christians settled. Many settled along Strangford Lough. In 2014 we moved to Portaferry. It is along this ancient pathway. I joined a cross community group that prays in Portaferry.

It is a beautiful place to live. On cloudless mornings the sun rose over the hill and forest to our left and lit up the sky, sometimes yellow, other times bright pink. As the morning progressed the sun rose higher in the sky and shone directly into our large kitchen. Light reflected off the Lough water and gave brightness and warmth. My healing continued in Portaferry.

AFTER CANCER

$\mathcal{M}$y healing from cancer in 2010 proved to me that Jesus loves me. No other power could heal me totally from fourth stage cancer. By shedding His blood on Calvary Jesus paid for my healing and delivered me from death. By His wounds I was healed. I was happy to be alive to finish rearing our children. Isaac, Abraham and Angela who were still at home. Life returned to normal after the difficult year of 2010.

Brendan wrote a book about my healing. *Staying Alive* was published in 2011. Alexandra Caldow from South Africa came to stay with us. She was sent by God to help me recover from the trauma of having had cancer. I had to rear my family with its challenges. She prayed with me every day, encouraged me when I was down, and helped with household chores.

She was a friend to the children who hadn't left home yet. We resumed a meeting in our home every Friday night to praise and thank God for His care and healing. I was blessed that God sent someone to help me. In nine months I was feeling stronger. Alexandra returned home to South Africa. Like the swallows she came in the spring-time and returned in the autumn.

Brendan and I looked after Isaac, Abraham and Angela in the next few years. Isaac went to Ulster University in Jordanstown. Abraham went to St Andrew's. In 2014 Angela left home to go to Edinburgh University.

We now had an empty nest! There were no more fledglings left! They had grown up and had moved on from their parents. It was lonely after all the activity of a full household. Instead of children running up and down the stairs all I heard was the emptiness.

In Downpatrick we settled in a home that was once owned by Oliver Cromwell's niece. It was one of the earliest buildings in Downpatrick. The house is in Saul Street, named after Saul where St Patrick settled.

Mature trees filled the bottom of the garden. Its hedgerows provided homes for blackbirds, doves, robins, thrush and sparrows. Blossoms on the laburnum, magnolia and rhododendron trees signalled spring. We flourished in our new home. Brendan liked our home in Saul Street, the wooden windows and shutters, the wide wooden stairs, his office where he wrote his books and the nearness to the town and schools.

We all enjoyed breakfast or coffee in the front garden when the morning sun shone. The children came down one by one. We chatted and relaxed. We had barbecue's, birthdays and conversations around campfires. There was champagne on the lawn for our guests at our son John's wedding to Rachel.

The heating was turned off in some of the rooms. Where there used to be life, chatter, laughter, lights on and essays being written, there was silence and a chill in the air. There was no one to call, to make a cup of tea and have a chat. There was no news about what friends were up to.

There was no cries of "Who touched my Razor." "Where is my toothbrush?" "Who used my hair gel?" "Dinner is ready!" "It's now prayer time."

There were five levels of stairs in our home so one had to shout loud. Even then everyone did not hear the call for dinner. There was often silence when I called for help in the kitchen. An Ethiopian Apostle called Kebede came to visit us. Brendan wrote a book for him called *A Man Of Ethiopia*. Kebede enjoyed the buzz in our home. It reminded him of his own country where there is always plenty of activity and noise.

The jam in the cupboard grew mould because there was no-one to eat peanut and jam sandwiches. I threw out vegetables and leftovers in the fridge because there was no hungry boys coming in from football to eat them.

The washing machines were silent. There were usually two washing machines on the go to wash towels and all the jeans and socks. There were no football bags in the corridor to trip over. I don't have to replace many toilet rolls. There was no smell of burnt toast. The kitchen sink was not full of dirty saucepans. All the signs of life were gone.

The house was warmer when all the bodies were in the house. The children did their chores on a Saturday morning. There was help to keep fires lit and logs cut. I loved the sound of the hoover on the landing. The carpets were being refreshed. Now the dust gathers and we don't see it. Cobwebs grow on the window shutters.

A proverb says,

> "Where there are no cattle the stall is empty
>   but with increase of oxen there is
>   strength."[1]

The grass grew longer. Weeds flourished in the plant pots. Hedgerows needed attention. The swing that Brendan and John attached to a branch high up in a fir tree hung silent. No more squealing from grandchildren who flew high above the trees. Outside our kitchen was a sheltered and sunny area. We had lunch there or our evening meal when it was warm. We lingered there many evenings to watch the sun go down.

The work is too much for just two of us. Reluctantly Brendan and I have agreed to downsize. We have to leave this old house that has lovingly protected us and our children for thirteen years. It has been a shelter from the wind and rain.

Its gardens provided play areas for our children and their friends and grandchildren, soil to grow my vegetables, trees to climb and a swing to dangle from. We are moving on before all the spring activity starts and I will be tempted to stay. I remember Shaking Stevens singing an old song,

> This old house once knew my children
> This old house once knew my wife
> This old house was home and comfort
> As we fought the storms of life
>
> This old house once rang with laughter
> This old house heard many shouts,
> Now he trembles in the darkness
> When the lightening walks about.
>
> Ain't going to need this house no longer
> Ain't going to need this house no more,
> Ain't got time to fix the shingles
> Ain't got time to fix the floor
>
> Ain't got time to oil the hinges
> Nor to mend the window panes,
> Ain't going to need this house no longer
> He's getting ready to meet his fate.

My hairdresser, Rosaleen told us about a modern house in Bright. We rented it and stored furniture we couldn't take with us. Soon afterwards David and Isaac left to live in Canada.

Between 2011 and 2013 six of our children moved to other nations. Hannah to Uganda for two and a half years. Mary to Ethiopia for a year. Patrick to Australia for two years and David and Isaac to Canada. Aaron moved to Slovakia with his family.

Brendan was regularly visiting his mother who in hospital. She died aged 94 later in the year. It was a sad time for us all. I was going through the trauma of my children leaving home for good.

Brendan was never happy in Bright. Seven months later we moved to Ballyhenry House in Portaferry. Instead of downsizing we upsized.

Our new home overlooked Strangford Lough and had lots of space, big gardens, raised beds for vegetables, a workshop and a large kitchen with an Aga cooker. It was more than we hoped for. It had enough space to accommodate our children and grandchildren. Our eldest son Brendan and his wife Tamara and their three lovely daughters, Maia, Rebecca and Stella were the first to visit.

THE BLACKBIRD MAKES
HIS NEST

*P*salm 84 says even the birds build a nest to rear their young near God's altar. Coleraine, Downpatrick and Portaferry were places where people prayed in unity; there was an altar of prayer.

We had the routine of praying with our children every night at bedtime. Jesus said where two or three gather in my name there am I in the midst of them.[1] Jesus was present with us as we prayed. Our children grew up in an atmosphere of God's presence. Brendan and I might have had strong disagreements, but God always restored us to continue to pray.

Our bathroom in Saul Street looked out onto mature trees. Their branches were at eye level with the window. Brendan noticed a pair of thrushes building a nest in one of the trees. They were easily seen working away before the leaves appeared. We watched their progress as they built their nest and reared their young.

There were so many blackbirds in our garden in Saul Street that I wanted to call our home 'Blackbird Cottage'. Every spring they competed for the best territory to build a nest. The hedgerows, the ivy covering the walls, the holly bushes, the under-growth of briars, all offered a safe place to build a nest.

In our large garden the birds could forage for food under fallen leaves or in some dead wood to feed their hungry chicks. Blackbirds had plenty to eat in spring and winter. It was an ideal habitat.

The male blackbird has black feathers and a bright orange beak. He is distinctive with his shiny coat as he sits on a branch surveying where he is planning to build his nest and singing to attract his female. She is close by, proud of her mate who is going to prepare a home for her and her young.

A pair of blackbirds built their nest in our garden in Captain Street, Coleraine. Brendan was laying paving stones and renovating the garden there. It took him a few weeks. While he was working with our children, the birds reared their young.

Now in Saul Street, Downpatrick another pair of blackbirds begin to build a nest in the thick hedge of our front garden. They fly in through a hole in the hedge with beaks full of small twigs, moss or wool. These make a cosy lining to keep mother and chicks warm. When the young are hatched father blackbird is even busier collecting food and feeding the young. He is working all the hours of sunlight.

The activity of the male blackbird reminds me of Brendan rearing our own young. Like the blackbird he was busy being responsible for me, his family and property. He made sure his home was warm and there was enough food. He had a house full of hungry young as well. He kept the home fires burning in the cold months.

Our new home in Portaferry has plenty of space for our children and grandchildren to visit. Even though our chicks have all flown the nest Brendan like the blackbird is still going to and fro putting things in place, hanging pictures of the children, making up beds, preparing his workplace, carrying chairs and tables.

He still sits at the head of the table as we share food and family times again. He will also sit around the camp fire out on the veranda and tell stories to his grandchildren. Stories he told to his own children.

People have often asked us 'How did you afford such a big family?' We had faith in God like the birds. He will care for us. We are more important than the birds. God promised to care for us. He is worthy to be trusted.

Even the sparrow finds a home, and the
swallow builds her nest and raises her
young at a place near your altar, O Lord
of Heaven's Armies, my King and my
God.[2]

NEWS FROM HOME

I was inspired to write about where I live after reading "Sweet Killough let down your Anchor", written by Maurice Hayes. Maurice's mother was born in Listowel, Co Kerry. Living in Killough at the other end of Ireland seemed a million miles away in the 1930s. Maurice's grandmother sent his young mum a copy of the Kerryman every week. News from home kept her in touch with her own county.

My children live in different parts of the world so writing my blogs gives them a flavour of our life in Portaferry, beside Strangford Lough.

There is a bay in front of our home, sheltered by the forest on one side and Ballyhenry Island on the other. When the sun shines this area becomes a warm haven. Stars of light dance on the water. When Brendan and I take a walk, we see the wildlife along the seashore, in the water, in the air or on the nearby grasslands. Each morning is different.

We enjoyed having our feet on the ground again after our recent trip to Slovakia. We heard a honking sound from the other side of the lough. There were swans flying in formation. Swans migrate from Iceland at this time of the year and fly south. I hope like us they get a rest after their long journey.

Brendan counted fourteen swans, the number of our children. All our children have left home. Gone but not forgotten. This day fifty years ago I gave birth to our first child, Shann. So started many years of child rearing.

A group of oystercatchers sprang into flight giving out their noisy shrill call. These birds feed along the shore on insects and molluscs. They have black and white feathers with a long orange beak. We disturbed them as we approached. They were hardly noticeable along the water's edge, camouflaged by the dark stones and sea weed. Herons and oyster-catchers live happily together along the shore. A black backed gull intimidated a heron standing on the water's edge. Gulls try to chase herons, much to their annoyance and screech their disapproval as they fly off.

A lone curlew catches Brendan's attention. He takes a closer look with the binoculars. It has a distinctive long curved bill. My little book of birdwatching comes in handy.

A large bird of prey bird dropped speedily into a field

nearby. It later perched on the top branch of a tree in the hedge row in the distance. We could see markings on its back feathers. We knew it was a bird of prey, but which one? I looked up my little book.

It was a kestrel.

EVERY MAN NEATH HIS VINE
AND FIG TREE

I have been inspired by scriptures that talk about homes. I read that when King Solomon reigned in Judah and Israel, the people

> "Were very contented with plenty to eat and
> drink. And there was peace throughout
> the entire land. They lived in peace and
> safety. Each family had his own home
> and garden."[1]

During the troubles in Northern Ireland we had little sense of peace and safety. People were suspicious of one another. There was tension in the air. Skies were grey. There was little sunshine. I longed for the days of sunshine and safety.

The Troubles ended with the Good Friday Peace Agreement in 1998. The fighting with guns and bombs stopped. The Agreement changed the atmosphere in Northern Ireland. There came a new freedom spiritually for us. Where doors were closed for us before a new door to move opened. It was dark. That same year we moved from Coleraine to Co. Down. It was a time of change. The tension in the country lifted. We had our own home and garden.

February 2020 brought new restrictions to us. The Covid Pandemic started in the UK. It was a flu like disease that affected one's breathing. Many people died from it globally. The government put restrictions in place to help prevent the rapid spread of the disease.

Schools, hotels, factories and non essential work stopped. Families had to stay at home. If one had a garden it was a great bonus. Friends were allowed to visit in the garden.

When I travel in Mediterranean countries I admire the little white houses with the families sitting under the shade of the vine tree in the cool of the evening. It is a picture of what I read in Scripture,

"And every man neath his vine and fig tree
shall live in peace and be unafraid."[2]

I enjoy the house and gardens at Ballyhenry House. The beauty all around brings healing to my mind and emotions. As the days get longer and warmer it is pleasant to sit outdoors and enjoy the view of the lough, the flowers, birds singing and fresh air. It is good for the soul and body. I enjoy sitting outdoors in the morning sun having coffee. It is not as warm as Greece. There is no grape vine but it is still good to be outdoors.

I am in touch with nature and the seasons. I see snow-drops when they appear in January, a sign of longer and brighter days. The green shoots of daffodils appear above ground in February. The yellow trumpet flowers sway in the spring breezes. The tulips appear in March.

God has been faithful to keep His promise to me of living in peace and being unafraid. I am enjoying the sunshine and safety in Portaferry.

THE FERRYMEN

I make boats from driftwood I find on the shore near where I live. The winter storms buffet and throw up broken pieces. I enjoy making something new and beautiful, a sailing boat ornament, from that which is discarded or broken. The reclaimed wood is now loved by its new owner as it sits on display in his home.

From the front of our home we look out on Strangford Lough. We see the Strangford-Portaferry ferry cross over the channel every fifteen minutes. I love to see the boat cross, regular as clock work from seven thirty am till eleven pm. When we take a trip into Downpatrick we take the ferry.

When we were moving from Bright to Portaferry one of the workers on the ferry said to my husband, 'You will soon own part of this ferry with all the money you are spending.' My daughter Hannah enjoys watching the ferry at night as its diesel engine chug chugs along. The ferry is company as she watches its lights as it moves to and fro across the lough.

There were storms this week. The ferry stills works even through gales, snow and chilling winds. Often the men's hands and faces are blue from the cold, as they collect the fare. The weather does not stop them being cheery and give a pleasant greeting.

The Portaferry~Strangford ferry is the biggest vessel in these parts. Portaferry had a history of building boats. A boat, St Brendan, build by a local man called John Murray takes visitors sightseeing up the lough.

A carol service is arranged at Christmas time on the ferry. It is lit up and the deck is a stage for choirs singing carols. Praise songs ring out over the Lough in the chilly, evening air. School children and adults take part. Drivers are entertained as they make their way home.

The ferry crossing between Strangford and Portaferry is the oldest continuous ferry crossing in the world! I can imagine Patrick and the early Christian settlers making the crossing back centuries ago in a wooden craft.

I have had some interesting events on my journeys across on the ferry. On returning from visiting relatives in Downpatrick I was the first in the queue to catch the evening eight o clock ferry from Strangford to Portaferry. I arrived just as the ferry was docking.

My children and I looked out and noticed the ferry boat was moving from side to side and not docking. I wondered what was happening. There was no strong wind blowing and the sea was calm.

I switched off my lights which were in full beam! The boat docked. The few cars and passengers disembarked. I moved forward onto the rampart and was about to park my car.

I was waved to a stop by an attendant. He waved his finger as he berated me for stopping the ferry docking. I didn't understand. He told me my lights were in full beam and because of this the ferry driver could not see to dock the boat.

He said, "Did you not read the notice that drivers are to turn off their lights!"

I apologised, realising I had "rocked the boat".

On another evening I arrived at the ferry terminal on time. The boat was full and the ferryman signalled to me, no more vehicles. I stopped, resigned to wait half an hour till the ferry returned.

I said a quick prayer, "Please Lord let the ferryman change his mind."

Just as I said that the ferryman asked drivers on deck to move forward to make room for another vehicle. He beckoned me forward.

I was excited at the quick answer to prayer. I was full of joy and thanked the men for their help in making room for me. The ferry boat launched forward. I saw the sky move and wondered what was happening. Then there was a crash.

My car had moved backwards and broke the long pole that is lifted and closed when cars get on and off the ferry. I was disoriented and in shock. In my excitement at getting on the ferry, I forgot to put the hand-brake on.

I was anxious on my journey across the lough. I wondered, What will the staff think when they see the broken pole crash at the back of the boat! I have damaged the ferry boat. Perhaps I should have stayed at home and not bothered going out to help a friend.

I remembered a promise from Psalm 121,

I will watch over your going in and out".[1]

I said another quick "Please help me" prayer to God. I waited as other cars started up their engines, preparing to disembark when we got to the other side.

Then one staff member discovered the damage. He called to another. Three or four men gathered to look at the fallen barrier. I waited in trepidation.

There was no scolding. No rebuke. In fact they laughed at what had happened. Thankfully they waved me forward and off the boat. They will take care of it. No calling the police to the scene of an accident. Thank God for the ferrymen who helped me.

One cold blustery night I was returning home. I was racing down the road from Downpatrick to Strangford. I arrived at the ferry terminal. I was comfortable in my warm car and looking forward to a glowing coal fire back home. The boat had just left. When the driver saw me he returned to the slipway and let down the passageway to let me drive on.

A few other times my car has lost power and wouldn't start when I should have drove off. One of the ferrymen helped me with jump leads to start my car again.

The ferrymen provide a great service. They are always friendly and helpful. I thank them all, especially Chris and Shane.

SPRING VISITORS

$\mathscr{O}$n Easter Sunday the sun was shining. Many families were out for a drive. The two ferry boats between Portaferry and Strangford were racing across the Narrows to help the travellers on their day out; perhaps to visit the festivities at Castleward, Castlewellan or Newcastle. People come from Strangford to visit the Aquarium in Portaferry or take a tour of the Ards Peninsula.

Other visitors arrived on the lough. A beautiful tall yacht drew up within my view. The owners were getting it ready for sailing events over the summer. I watched as it was secured to a buoy.

It is the season for yachtsmen to put their vessels back in the water. A crane will lift the boats, which look like big birds, and settle them on the water.

It's good to be alive and see life abundant all around. Jesus came to give us life and life abundantly.[1] He has done that for me. Sap is rising in the tree trunks. The leaves of the trees burst open and discard their shells. Sticky pollen from the sycamore tree is falling all around.

We took a drive a few days before to pick up our daughter Mary who returned for Easter. The water had filled Strangford Lough as far up as Newtownards. It reached up to the wall that separated the road from the sea. I looked down through the clear water as we drove along the shore. Where else is there a place where one can drive for miles so close to the shore? I was enjoying the still waters that restore my soul.

Easter Monday is memorable for me. Thirteen years ago I went to the Accident and Emergency in the local town. I was later diagnosed with fourth stage cancer. Praise God I am staying alive after my experience with cancer. I celebrated the victory over the weekend with my family.

On Tuesday the weather changed. Grey clouds rolled in on stormy winds from the west. There was a chill in the air. Warm coats were worn again. All the visitors had gone. They returned home revived and refreshed from having time out in the country.

Today, there are other newcomers. The swallows have arrived for the summer. They nest under the eaves and rear their young. They waste no time. A couple of them inspected the nest used last year and began mending it, flying in and out with mud in their beaks.

All the ways of nature have a purpose. The swallows

have travelled thousands of miles from Africa. The strong south east winds helped them on their way.

The same winds carried the Brent Geese north on their return journey to Canada. I miss them. I miss their loud calls as they gathered beneath our garden to drink from the fresh stream.

I'll enjoy the company of the swallows over the summer along with the resident forest and sea birds. The blackbirds, robins, pigeons, pheasants, doves, thrush, starlings and sparrows are busy making nests for their young. The call of the doves in the morning replace the Brent Geese. The other birds join the chorus. The time of singing of birds has come. [2]

GUILLEMOTS

*T*he Black Guillemot is a small sea bird. His black, smooth feathers and pointed black beak, make it easy for him to glide underwater and feed on mollusks. He has bright red legs and a patch of white on each wing.

Guillemots live at sea most of the time but return to rear their young at suitable nesting sites. Portaferry is a place for Guillemots. There is a nest for one couple in the wall near where we live. Every year they build their nest in a crevice above the water line on this stone wall. The south facing wall receives the full warmth of the sun, a comfortable place to get the maximum heat for their vulnerable young chicks. They are hidden from the blast of chilly winds and out of reach of predators.

This pair is quite tame. They rear three young. Passers-by stop to watch them as their family play in the water below, diving, splashing, ducking, or flying up to test their wings. As I was driving past one evening two birds were sitting on the wall. I stopped to see them up close. The two birds didn't fly off. I took some photos. Seeing the Guillemots reminded me of God's faithfulness to me in providing safe warm places for me to rear our young.

The waves from storms in February 2020 breached the sea wall in various places along Loughshore Road in Portaferry. The road was closed to traffic. These seasonal storms coincided with the bigger storm of Covid 19. The country was in lockdown. People had to work from home and stay home. They were allowed to walk locally for exercise or to walk their pets. The Loughshore Road became busier than usual.

Much damage happened to the walls of Loughshore Road that spring. Walls were built up again and the road below our driveway was renewed. Our neighbour filled in pot holes along the lane. I was reminded of the verse in Isaiah. God promises to rebuild the ruins. He will rebuild our walls. If we feel damaged by waves of adversity God will heal, restore and repair that which is broken in our lives. He was doing that for me. [1]

Beyond Ballyhenry Island the sea wall collapsed and part of the road fell into the sea. In July when work was due to start to repair the road, it was discovered that a group of black guillemots had built nests in the wall near the break in the roadway. They were still feeding their young in the nests.

The Department of the Environment wisely stepped in and advised work to stop. The repair didn't go ahead till all the birds had left.

THE PRINCESS CUP

Sara Joye said "Grandma, I want to buy a Princess cup for my teacher."

"What is a Princess cup?"

"You know, like your cups, Grandma."

She pointed to some china cups with flowered patterns on them in my cupboard.

"Don't you have these in Slovakia?"

"No grandma, only in your house."

"So you want to get a special patterned cup and saucer for your teacher?"

"Yes, I just love Princess cups".

Sara Joye held a china cup in her hands close to her heart as if it was the most beautiful, tender thing in the world.

I enjoy collecting jugs and china plates with flowers and gold trim on them. I use them for tea when friends visit. I display them on my dressers in the kitchen.

I remember *The Old Woman of the Roads* by Padraic
Colum.

O, to have a little house!
To own the hearth and stool and all!
The heaped up sods against the fire,
The pile of turf against the wall!

To have a clock with weights and chains
And pendulum swinging up and down!
A dresser filled with shining delph,
Speckled and white and blue and brown!

I could be busy all the day
Clearing and sweeping hearth and floor,
And fixing on their shelf again
My white and blue and speckled store!

I could be quiet there at night
Beside the fire and by myself,
Sure of a bed and loth to leave
The ticking clock and the shining delph!

Och! but I'm weary of mist and dark,
And roads where there's never a house nor
    bush,
And tired I am of bog and road,
And the crying wind and the lonesome
    hush!

And I am praying to God on high,
And I am praying Him night and day,
For a little house - a house of my own
Out of the wind's and the rain's way.

I had a dream after we moved to our seven bedroom home in Downpatrick. I was thinking about the cost of heating this new home in winter. In the dream I saw a pile of turf, a pile of logs and a pile of coal stacked against the wall of our new home.

The picture was just like in the poem, the pile of turf. God was reassuring me there will be a plentiful supply of heating fuel. God has been faithful. He looks after us like he does the birds. He still supplies my need for heating in our big house in Portaferry. The home fire shines bright in the hearth and the blue delph shines on the dresser.

I always wanted a dresser to display pottery, fine china, glasses or gifts, high up out of little children's reach. In my new home I have two dressers. Items, I collected over the years are now on display. Chinese patterned plates, I received as twenty fifth anniversary present, wine glasses, china plates, gifts from my children and family photos. My dream has come true. My collection is being added to regularly as I pick up bargains from a car boot sales or craft markets. Now my grandchildren admire my collection.

On Saturday my son Aaron, Marta and their children went to shop locally. I wondered would Sara Joye find any Princess cups. Her Mum prayed. "Dear Lord please let someone bring Princess cups to the Charity shop today."

They set off. Some time later they called for me to give them a lift home. It was cold and raining but the children's spirits were not dampened. Instead there was great excitement. Princess cups were purchased at a bargain price. It happened just as Marta had prayed. In an Antique store or Fine China shop these goods would be costly. The prized purchases were carefully wrapped to keep them safe on the journey back to Slovakia.

The old woman of the roads didn't have her dream come true, but I did.

> May he grant you your heart's desires and
> make all your plans succeed. [1]

BEAUTIFUL MOSAICS

*a*s time passed in Portaferry I was feeling rested and refreshed. I was inspired to make mosaics after picking up broken pieces of glass and pottery from Portaferry beach. This helped continue my healing from sad and bad times. You can read about our lives in our books, *Staying Alive* and *The Grapes are Worth It.*

One sunny morning in springtime I went for a walk along the foreshore. It was a stony beach. I noticed pieces of green glass glistening among the pebbles. I picked up the pieces until my pocket was full. It felt like panning for gold along the shoreline. Brendan joined me in my treasure hunt. We collected lots of clear glass alongside shades of blue, green, and brown.

I inspected them when I returned home. I asked myself what can I do with these colourful but broken pieces of glass. The edges weren't sharp any more and their colours were cloudy from years of sea storms. The pieces reminded me of what happens to a person in the storms of life. Troubles, disappointments, or rejection leaving one relegated to the ash heap. When washed and cleansed my pieces of glass were ready to be made into something beautiful.

As I looked at the different shapes of green pieces, I was inspired to make my first mosaic. I found a piece of wood and a tube full of tile filler. This was my first piece of Art. I'd not been aware about sea glass before.

On Saturday I discovered a new site along the shore-line to build up my supply of broken pieces. I added to my collection, pieces of pottery. I was excited to see how these pieces would clean up. Some had blue willow patterns, some had pink and green colours. The pieces of glass and pottery on the beach were all that remains of once useful and valued vessels.

Perhaps the blue glass was once a beautiful perfume bottle or the piece of pottery, a treasured piece of willow patterned delph on a housewife's dresser. How would they fit into a mosaic? I have made many beautiful mosaics since; birds, angels, cottages, trees and others.

I attend local craft fairs. My new hobby brings me joy and satisfaction. I can work at home in my workshop. My son John who is a sculptor helped me cut pieces of wood . I find I relax as I work. My mind is being healed from past trauma. I'm not worrying about my children.

As I work, I remember glass is made from the common material, sand. The sand is heated to 1700 degrees. Through the fire sand changes to become glass. Pottery is made from clay, a common material. The clay is treated in high temperatures to turn it to pottery.

The Word of God tells us that we were created by God from the dust of the earth. We are the clay, you are the potter; we are all the work of your hand.[1] When I go through difficult times I often wonder what is happening to me. I feel like the clay in the fire being changed into pottery or the sand being made into glass. This passage from Peter explains,

> "Dear friends, do not be surprised at the
>> fiery ordeal that has come on you to test
>> you, as though something strange were
>> happening to you. [2]

In our lives our Creator God can reach down and touch all that remains of a broken vessel and make something new. My mosaics speak to me of hope. There is life after brokenness.

My mosaics can be displayed on a dresser once more or perhaps adorn a bathroom wall and be a thing of beauty again. God can restore our lives.

A FARMER PLOUGHING

*B*rendan and I walked through Nugent's Wood to have coffee and cake in our favourite Portaferry restaurant, *Deli-licious.*

Near the forest a farmer was ploughing a broad field that spreads across a hill and flows down to the sea wall. The seagulls were following the tractor. Every year this field produces a fruitful crop, be it rapeseed or wheat. It lies in the full light of the sun which warms the soil . The seeds sprout, grow and ripen.

When the full moon appears in March, the farmer knows it is time to plough up the ground. This moon is called the Worm Moon. That's when the worms come up nearer the surface of the soil after spending the winter in warmer depths. Their activity in the soil aerates it and prepares it to help the seed grow.

Seeing the farmer made me think of Joseph Campbell's poem,

I will go with my father a-ploughing
To the green field by the sea
And the rooks and the crows and the
      seagulls
Will come flocking after me
I will sing to the patient horses
And my father will sing the plough-song
That blesses the cleaving share.

The farmers of the past ploughed their fields with horse drawn ploughs. The farmer today is using a big tractor pulling a large wide machine which grinds up the soil. Hundreds of gulls follow the fresh upturned soil. They dive for tasty morsels of worms and insects disturbed by the machinery.

Rooks and crows from the forest join in the foray, just as the poem says. Joseph Campbell was born in Co. Down. Perhaps his father ploughed in the same green fields by the sea near where I live.

In the forest there are other signs of spring. The ferns are unfurling their wheels of tiny leaves. A green carpet of ferns and bluebell shoots spring up beneath the trees before the leaves appear above. The steep bank beside the path has a waterfall of bluebell blossoms. We take time to linger and enjoy.

Today I think of the verse where Jesus said,

"Here is an illustration of what the kingdom
      of God is like. A farmer planted seeds in a

field and then he went on with his other activities. As the days went by the seeds sprouted and grew without the farmers help, because the earth produces crops on its own. First a leaf pushes through, then the heads of wheat are formed and finally the grain ripens. And as soon as the grain is ready the farmer comes and harvests it.[1]

The seed Jesus mentions represents the Word of God that is shared with others. The farmer represents a person who shares the Word of God with others. In time the seed of the Word of God will grow up and bear fruit in the person who receives the Word.

I often share with others about my healing, through my blogs on Facebook, Wordpress or when I give away my book, *Staying Alive*. What God has done for me he can do for others. It is God who causes the seed to grow up in time and produce a harvest. I do not worry how someone responds to what I say. My work is to share with others that Jesus heals.

> Who causes the the grass, flowers and trees
> to bud and blossom? For as the soil
> makes the sprout come up and a garden
> causes seeds to grow, so the Sovereign
> Lord will make righteousness and praise
> spring up before all.[2]

THE BRENT GEESE

The Brent Geese fly to Strangford Lough from Northern Canada in September every year. They come in their thousands. I heard their call in the distance on the sixth of September when I was out for a walk. I looked up and saw a chevron of them making their way towards the Lough. The birds have flown many miles from distant shores to get to these feeding grounds on Strangford Lough.

They look like ducks when they arrive. They spend the next eight months in Ireland feeding on eel grass, which grows on the intertidal shore especially where fresh water meets the salt water.

In April groups of geese gather near our home to feed and drink from the fresh water stream. I can hear their guttural calling. They are fattening up for their flight across the ocean. They now look like geese.

They waddle from where they are feeding to the shore

and float away on the water when they are disturbed. They conserve energy at this stage only flying off when in danger. When they do take flight they travel very fast just above the level of the water and disappear into the distance.

The geese have strengthened themselves for the return journey to have their young in Canada. They fly north beyond Greenland to a place called Polar Bear Pass.

I am filled with wonder as I consider the rhythm of their lives. They stay together feeding and flying. There is safety in numbers. They go for miles to find safe places to feed and return to Canada where there are no enemies, to rear their young. Isn't it amazing the timing in nature? These birds have been migrating since creation. How marvellous our Creator is.

The geese's feather colours are dark on the neck and wings. Their wing tips and underbelly are white. When the sun shines the light highlights the white feathers, making the birds look regal with the black and white contrast.

The Irish Brent Research Group tells me the parents remain with the young for fifteen months before the fledglings are strong enough to make the long journey to feeding grounds along the shores of Ireland. They care for their young. Even the birds follow the truth in the scripture, "He gently leads those who are with young."[1]

The migrating geese leaving en masse signify a powerful force in nature. They know when the time is right. When the strong winds arrive in April groups of geese gather and take off north. The desire to leave and return are part of the bird's life cycle.

These small creatures do gigantic feats. They fly thousands of miles from here to another continent. They arrive at the right time and leave at the right time. Many of the species of birds that come to Strangford Lough have come here for generations.

I believe St Brendan set out west into the Atlantic Ocean without knowing what was across the waves. Perhaps watching the birds may have inspired him to search. The swans and Brent Geese come to Ireland every September and leave again in Spring. Where do they go to?

St Brendan set sail by boat and flowed with the currents of the North Atlantic drift. It took him north to Scotland, the Shetlands and the Orkney Islands. He continued west with the current and came to Iceland. He travelled further west and reached Canada. I am inspired by St Brendan's voyage. As the Bible says,

> Even the stork that flies across the sky
> knows the time of her migration, as do
> the turtledove, the swallow, and the
> crane. They all return at the proper time
> each year.[2]

TRAVELLING TO THE NATIONS

atching the birds flying back to Strangford Lough each year reminds me that Brendan and I are like the birds. We travel back and forth to nations that have opened up to us. Like the Brent Geese and the Redshank we go to Canada and Iceland.

It was after all our fourteen children were born that God led Brendan to travel. Someone said you will never have a ministry if you have so many children. Yet we believed the prophetic word that Brendan would travel to the nations. I stayed home and looked after the children while Brendan traveled. After they left home, I was free to travel with Brendan.

Early Christians settled along the shores of Strangford Lough at Nendrun, Greyabbey and Movilla. I can imagine the early settlers coming ashore like the Brent Geese to get fresh water after their long sea journey. Perhaps they built a shelter and fished from the sea that was teeming with fish in those early days. No pollution or overfishing then.

St Patrick's writings mention scriptures, dreams, the Father, Son and Holy Ghost. The Christian denominations all look to St Patrick as their patron saint in Ireland. We are united in the heritage St Patrick left us since the sixth century.

Ireland is known as the Land of Saints and Scholars. Many missionaries travelled from these shores into Europe, Africa, Asia, Australia and the Americas bringing the Good News about Jesus. Today Brendan and I go on mission to different countries, praying for healing and encouraging with prophetic words and interpretation of dreams.

I have travelled with Brendan to New Zealand, Indonesia, Israel, India, Sri Lanka, Mediterranean countries, the United Kingdom, Iceland, America and Canada. I enjoyed my travels but I am so happy to return home to Ireland.

It is comforting to hear the accent of the air hostesses on the flight back to Belfast or listen in to Hugo Duncan's cheery radio show. I don't mind the mist over Strangford Lough, the gentle rain, or the odd storm and winds that leaves a salty spray on my windows.

After university two of my sons, David and Isaac settled in Canada. David went to Toronto and Isaac moved to Vancouver. I was sad when they left home to live so far away. But as parents we have to let our children fly the nest. When I see the Brent Geese return every

September I often wonder will any of my sons return to Ireland.

In 2020, Covid hit the world. People's lives changed. Many people weren't allowed to travel or work. Isaac and Simone in Vancouver had three young children. Isaac worked from home and lived in a basement flat. All recreation facilities closed down. They couldn't visit family or friends. They decided to return to Ireland.

Like the Brent Geese one day Isaac and his family returned to live in Ireland. I was heart broken when Isaac left home but full of joy when he returned with his wife Simone and their three sons, Benjamin, John and Lochlan. God fulfilled his promise to me that my son would return from afar.[1] [2]

MY BIRTHDAY

*I*n May, it was my birthday. I wanted to share with others in my town what God had done for me in healing me from fourth stage cancer.

My neighbour Rita lived on the farm beside us since she got married. I often called to visit. She told me many stories about life on the farm, rearing her children and working in Portaferry.

One day when I called she looked sad. She told me her grandson's wife Ellie was diagnosed with a fast growing type of breast cancer. She was just thirty years old with two girls. Rita is very proud of her six great grand daughters.

Her son and wife were heart broken. I reassured Rita that Jesus healed me from cancer. I said, Let's pray and ask God to heal this young mother. Other people were already praying for her. God healed Ellie. She had another child, a healthy baby boy, who is Rita's first great grandson.

Many people in Portaferry are a blessing to me. The ones who serve in the hotel, Captain Jacks, the hair-dressers, supermarkets, post office, and clinics are very welcoming. Joe's chippy is the best. He stays open till late. Ellen runs a charity shop. She helped me give out my books. Ellen is a great story teller.

Maureen welcomed me to a coffee morning in the Methodist Church. Through her and her husband Doug I joined a cross community prayer group. *Presence* is a group that works to promote unity among Christians and welcomes visitors during Gala Week. Matthias is a Puppeteer from Germany. He helps during Gala week.

I love the breakfast tea room Deli-licious. They make the freshest breakfast. The jam buns are a treat. The owner looks out for those in need. Some years previous Brendan and I visited the shop. There was a sign outside the door advertising fourteen flavours of ice cream. We had a photo taken beside the sign. Brendan and I produced fourteen flavours in our fourteen children.

I met Grainne in Deli-licious. She helps me do my housework after I fell from a pear tree and broke my wrist. She has the rooms and bathrooms shining in no time. My friends, Jimmy and Linda stayed in Portaferry for a few months while they waited to get a permanent home in Newcastle. Jimmy's mum came from Portaferry. They are a big encouragement to me.

Brendan suggested I call the priest, Father Fergal Mc Grady and tell him about my healing. I contacted Father Fergal and gave him my book. We shared many similar

interests. He was from a big family. He has been to Slovakia. He was thinking of working in Iceland.

Father Feargal got back to me on the Monday. He was
enthusiastic about what he had read. He invited me to
share my story at the Masses the following weekend. It
was Pentecost Sunday. I was happy to share about what
Jesus had done for me to all the parishioners.

I got to sow seeds of hope that God heals. What Jesus
has done for me he can do for others. I believe that Jesus
died on the cross to forgive sins and heal diseases and
restore lives. By His stripes we are healed.[1]

BIRD WATCHING FROM MY KITCHEN WINDOW

*T*oday is one of those days promised long ago. "You will see many good days." [1]

I am bird watching from the comfort of my warm kitchen. It is relaxing to sit quiet. Looking at the birds is taking my mind off work. My breakfast dishes need washed, benches need cleared and the floor needs brushed. Emails need checked. I have to make phone calls. But all can wait.

I don't have to go for a drive to a special bird watching sight, or get wrapped up in warm clothes to face the elements. It is a windless, clear morning. The sun is shining making stars dance on the sea beneath me in the bay.

There is a walled garden to the back of our home. It is flanked on three sides by a ten foot wall. These protect us from the wind but keep the warmth of the sunshine trapped in the garden. God promises in his Word to make us like a well-watered garden with walls around it. [2] God is our walls keeping trouble and evil out.

There are many birds in my garden this morning. A Great Tit is singing from the treetop. He wants to attract a female to share his domain. A pair of doves rest on a branch cooing. A wren stays low along the hedge. A robin jumps about among the plant pots looking for insects. A blackbird turns over leaves near the vegetable bed. They live at peace with each other.

A starling was inspecting a hole in the wall where a family of starlings had been reared last year. He is preparing for this year's brood. There are two pairs of starlings flying back and forth. They each have found a nook in the old garden wall. One bird flies in with a small twig in his mouth. He didn't exit for five minutes. He must be building his nest, even though it is still early in the year. I look forward to watching their progress each morning.

Robins, wrens, blackbirds, wagtails, starlings and chaffinches live in our walled garden. They don't chase each other or compete for territory. Can't it be the same for us living in Northern Ireland? There is space for everyone to live together without war.

> How good and pleasant it is when brothers
>   dwell together in unity.
> For there The Lord commands his blessing.[3]

SWALLOWS ARRIVE FROM
AFRICA

esterday I noticed a pair of swallows swirling overhead. They are harbingers of spring in the northern countries of the world. They have arrived to rear their young. They have flown here thousands of miles from South Africa. This couple have come to nest where their family nested last year, and their families before them. It is in the eaves of the barn near us.

Such a small bird can fly such a long way. The birds inspected the nest left behind from last season. They fly off to collect soft mud to repair the outside of the nest. They will gather some soft moss or wool to line the nest. Three or four eggs are laid and kept warm by each bird brooding till the eggs are hatched. Then the swallows will spend most of their days flying through the air catching insects to feed their young

The swallow builds its nest near humans. When I lived at home on my father's farm, each year swallows would arrive. They flitted in and out of the barn bringing material for the nest or food for their young.

Sometimes I have to frighten away starlings that sit on the top of the barn waiting to rob the swallows' young from the nest below. After one batch are reared the adult birds start over again and rear another nest of young. They keep feeding them until September. Then they all gather on the local electric wires and fly off to Africa for the winter.

I watched a nature program about the flights of migrant birds. On the swallows' journey up north they stop off at different points to feed and rest for the next stage. One stopover is by a lake. The swallows arrive there, just when millions of flies hatch out. The air is dark with the flies. The swallows swoop in and out of the cloud of flies and have a feast.

This is an example of God providing for the birds of the air. I rejoice to see God's timing and provision for the birds of the air. Our creator and Father looks after all of his creation.

The swallows have no luggage, no belongings, no passport. They are free to fly over borders and nations. They are no threat to anyone. God had prepared a place for them in the barn behind our house.

In February of 2020 in the midst of Covid our son Abraham returned from London and our daughter Angela returned from Belfast. They climbed the hill behind our home to view the sunsets over Co. Down and they swam in the sea below. It was refreshing for them after living in the city.

In April of 2020 we celebrated Brendan's seventieth birthday. Covid restricted our numbers, yet a few of us gathered in the garden with a barbecue. There was no restriction on the birds coming to Brendan's birthday. The newly arrived swallows twittered as they swooped overhead.

> Even the stork that flies across the sky
> knows the time of her migration, as do
> the turtledove, the swallow, and the
> crane. They all return at the proper time
> each year.[1]

FUN IN BOATS

*M*y husband Brendan enjoys boats. Our first purchase of a boat was from a doctor in Portrush, who said he enjoyed many good days with his children and the boat on the local strand.

We also spent many happy days with the red and white boat in the shallow water of the River Foyle. We owned a couple of old caravans on Magilligan Beach. It was a safe place for our young children to swim and use the boat. Brendan wrote a poem about this time. He called it, *The Minibus Family*.

> Tuna de Beano, wooden spoons and love.
> Warm beds, dry houses, poems and prayers
> and prophecy.
> Endless days on Magilligan strand, The
> Minibus Family,

Brown as berries and as healthy as rainbow
trout.

Remember the rowing boat for a hundred
pounds?
Small and white with red trim,
From a one line ad in the Chronicle?
The owner could still hear his kids squealing
with delight,
As he took my crumpled five pound notes

They'd splashed and paddled,
Making waves where Simmons had his West
Strand Visions.
The craft moved on but the images remained.

And our own kids, fast as hares and as
hungry as hounds,
Casting long shadows, as they ran and swam
our days away.

We baptised ourselves in our growing
freedom.
Once we lay like Hansel and Grettle on the
beach,
Watching sturdy gulls fly high,
Soaring for joy in their airy kingdom,
As Dylan dreamed and screamed,

"It's all over now Baby Blue."

We introduced our grandchildren to boating when they came to stay with us in Portaferry. Aaron had left a yellow pedalo and two canoes with us after he moved to Slovakia. Hannah and Angela are great swimmers. They took Maia, Rebecca, Stella, Shann Rose, Maggie, Eva May and Jean Luc out on the boats when they came to visit during the summer holidays.

I have great memories of the children boating. They were safe as Hannah, Angela or Abraham swam with them in the still water. Their squeals of delight echoed up the hill beside us.

They had hot showers and hot food. Our home was like a summer camp for children. Wet clothes and towels were left to be washed while dinner was served.

Our son John and his young family lived near us in Portaferry for a time. He used our workshop as a studio for his carvings. We got to see his children, Joseph, Daniel, Samuel and Jonathan a bit more often that our other grandchildren.

THE TERNS HAVE ARRIVED

*N*ature's winter slumber is awakened by the warm sun and the longer days of spring. Terns announce their arrival across the Narrows on Swan Island with excited squeals and calls. They have reached their destination after their long flight from Southern lands.

They are on time! There is plenty of fish in Strangford Lough to feed upon to recover their strength. They will prepare a place to have their young after a while.

Terns arrive in April to a small island off Strangford. Hundreds of them nest and rear their young. Their familiar noisy screeching call welcomes the visitor to the Strangford ferry, which connects with Portaferry on the other side of the Lough. Even though the island is only a few yards from the shore the terns are safe. No one is allowed to go to the island to disturb the nesting birds.

Swan Island is a rock outcrop a few yards from

Strangford harbour. They are safe from intruders across a short stretch of water, but near enough for the onlooker to enjoy their activities. Thousands of travellers on the Strangford ferry will get to see these terns up close over the summer. Some of the birds stand on the end of the gangway on the ferry as it crosses the Lough. They aren't shy of humans.

There are many pairs in the colony that nest and rear their young on the small island. They are very noisy. They rise up into the air together, screech, fight and swoop and fly off to feed. They catch small fish on the surface of the water. The same flock of terns return year after year. They leave at the end of the summer.

The average Arctic Tern lives about thirty years and travels around 1.5 million miles during its lifetime. It is famous for its migration; it flies from its Northern breeding grounds to the Antarctic and back again each year, the shortest distance between these areas being 12,000 miles. The long journey ensures that this bird sees two summers per year and more daylight than any other creature on the planet.

In Portaferry, I'm looking at many of the birds God created. I'm watching how the birds nest and produce their offspring just as God planned it.

> Then God said, "Let the skies be filled with
> birds of every kind." So God created
> every sort of bird—each producing
> offspring of the same kind. And God saw

that it was good. Then God blessed them, saying, "Be fruitful and multiply. Let the birds multiply on the earth." And evening passed and morning came, marking the fifth day."[1]

God's glory is seen in his creation. Who tells the tern to leave the warm climate to come north to the best conditions to rear their young?

EAGLES IN CANADA

*B*rendan and I have visited Vancouver, Canada often to encourage people we know there through praying for healing and prophecy. We visit different friends in Cloverdale, Coquitlam, Langley, Surrey, Hope, Abbotsford and West Vancouver. After working with different groups we get to go sight seeing. We were visiting Sechelt, a town on the Sunshine Coast off Vancouver. The only access to Sechelt is by ferry.

Someone shouted, "The salmon are running." In a small stream nearby we saw crowds of salmon swimming up the river to lay their eggs in the sandy water bed. We stood watching this phenomena for a long time.

The salmon's life work is over. They die soon after laying their eggs and their dead bodies flow downstream. It was a sobering sight to see. The salmon have returned from the open ocean and swam up rivers to get to their source to lay eggs to produce a new generation.

They have accomplished their circle of life and then die. I thought of Brendan and I rearing our children. That stage of our life has come to an end. Our last children are leaving home. What happens now. Do we die?. No we will not die. We will move on to the work we are to do in the next season.

We had another adventure with nature. Hundreds of bald headed eagles gathered in an area in the hills where there was easy access to food. There were eagles everywhere, perched in trees or flying overhead. We spent the afternoon eagle watching. Our host Ivan Fox is a great photographer. He got some stunning pictures of the eagles.

Most eagles in North America live in BC, Canada. Occasionally we'd see a couple flying near the city. But that day we were in eagle heaven. We saw an abundance of eagles, a reward for our journey across the land and ocean from home, eight thousand miles away.

Eagles rear two or three young in a nest of branches high up on a ledge or tree. When the young are old enough to fly the parents unsettle the nest. They begin to dismantle the nest one bit at a time until it is uncomfortable for the birds to remain. They have no choice but to fly off and make a life on their own.

On that visit to Sechelt I believe God was showing me I have to let my children fly the nest and not hold onto them. Like the salmon I have had my family. That season is over.

In middle age an eagle looses it feathers. It's beak and

talons become gnarled. It can't catch prey effectively so it will fast. The eagle goes off on its own and waits till its feathers regrow and its beak and talons are healed. I have often felt like the eagle. I become tired and weary and I need time out to recover.

> They shall mount up with wings as eagles;
> they shall run, and not be weary; and
> they shall walk, and not faint.[1]

SWANS

$\mathcal{I}$ was pleasantly surprised on Sunday evening when I was driving along the River Quoile. A group of swans in the river caught my attention. I stopped the car and scrambled out to investigate. I had never seen such a large flock of swans there before.

Young adult swans were having an evening together. Circling, resting, washing, dipping, sailing, hissing, eating, cleaning, chirping, doing things swans do. Apparently at these get togethers the young adults chose life partners and start a family the next spring. My husband and I met at a dance where young people met together. Many marriages came from these meeting places for young people.

Seeing those young swans reminded me that it is the natural process of life for young to leave their parents and meet other young people of their age. My grown children will start out in their lives and meet their life partner and start a family of their own.

It was timely for me to come upon this scene. I have to release my children after they leave home into their future. I can still pray for them and trust God to guide them. Didn't Brendan and I leave our parents and set off in life together. Life circumstances and pain guided us to look to the One who shows us how to live, our Heavenly Father.

Swans mate for life. About eight eggs are laid and hatched. In the Downpatrick area I have seen families of swans up to seven fully reared young. When the cygnets are a year old they leave the parents and join the flock of other single swans.

There are a couple of swans whose territory is along the river Quoile. Each year they raise young cygnets. People out for a walk bring food to feed them. It is a good place to rear their young. The walkers supplemented the cygnets diet. They grew strong and survived.

Years previous when several children were still at home, my son David commented that these swans reminded him of our family. Seven children still living at home needed reared. They too were growing strong and surviving well.

Watching the swans' cycle of life with their family helped me not to worry as I raised my own children. I have to release them to fly to start a new life. It's a painful process to release the family ties but it has to happen for our children to learn how to live and survive. I trust what our children learned from Brendan and I will help them on their life's journey.

> Train up a child in the way she should go
> and when he is old he will not depart
> from it.[1]

THE ROBIN

*E*lizabeth Cheney wrote,

> Said the robin to the sparrow,
> "I should really like to know,
> Why these anxious human beings
> Rush about and worry so."
> Said the sparrow to the robin,
> "Friend I think that it must be,
> That they have no Heavenly Father,
> Such as cares for you and me."

We have a faithful little Robin who lives in our garden. He does not fly away to other countries. He is a resident. When Brendan and I return from a trip the Robin flies over to greet us. Then he jumps from branch to branch making a fuss. In the wintertime when he is not busy rearing his young he comes in through the open door and jumps around the kitchen.

His territory extends to the back and front of our garden. He shares it with other birds but not with other robins. He has some nice territory to defend. He has two gardens in which to forage and get plenty of food for his offspring. Brendan leaves out bird seed for him every morning. He isn't going to give up easily. If another Robin comes to take over his patch he will defend it till his rival was defeated. I have noticed our little bird friend sitting on the fence with a few of his feathers ruffled.

What can I learn from this little bird?

Jesus said look at the birds.

This Robin is a real warrior fighting for his home and his land where he gets provision for his young. Man has the spiritual enemy Satan and his demons. Satan comes to rob, steal and destroy but Jesus comes to give us life and life abundantly. When we believe in Jesus He protects us from the power of Satan. Jesus changes me from the inside out as I continue to follow him. He sets us free from the oppression of the devil.

In Nehemiah 4:4 the Jewish men prayed for their families and their homes. They built with one hand and defended their property with a sword in their other hand.

Like the Robin I often get a few ruffled feathers as I defend my home and children. It is my space and I want to keep it a safe place free from evil.

Jesus warned us to continue to keep our house free from evil spirits. They will always want to come back in. They will never give up. So one needs to be on guard to prevent evil coming back into one's life once we have been set free. Keep believing, praying and reading God's word.

THE CHAFFINCH

*I*n springtime many birds come to our garden to eat the titbits my husband leaves for them. The food ranges from bread crumbs, left overs and bird-seed. Each bird is glad of any extra food to feed their fast growing young. I enjoy the company of our feathered friends, the robin, chaffinch, tits and wren. When the young have flown the nest and the weather turns cold many birds return to the bird table.

The Chaffinch is larger and more confident than other birds that visit. He is handsome with a blue-grey cap, reddish-brown breast and back. Brendan noticed he comes to feed when dark seeds are left out. He feeds on seed from the thistle, which is a thorny plant.

The chaffinch is sometimes associated with Christ's crown of thorns and His shed blood. I was glad to see this beautiful visitor on our fence in the morning especially after reading about the chaffinch's association with Our

Saviour. The grey feathers on his head is like the crown of thorns and his red breast reminds us of the blood that flowed down from Jesus wounds.

I thank God for Jesus. The crown of thorns pierced His head, blood flowed down His forehead and matted His hair. The flesh on His back was opened up with the thongs of a whip. His body and clothes were covered in blood from His wounds. Men turned away from the sight.

> "He had no beauty or majesty to attract us to
> him, nothing in his appearance that we
> should desire him. He was despised and
> rejected by mankind, a man of suffering,
> and familiar with pain. Like one from
> whom people hide their faces he was
> despised, and we held him in low esteem.
> But he was pierced for our transgressions, he
> was crushed for our iniquities; the
> punishment that brought us peace was
> on him, and by his wounds we are
> healed."[1]

POEMS

I will recite a lovely poem to the King for my tongue is the pen of a ready writer.[1]

THE OLD HERON WAITING

The tide is high in Strangford Lough
No room to wade on the shoreline
The water is lapping against the wall
I'm safe here on this stake
Jutting out of the water
My favourite spot
I'm too old to fly from my perch
To find another fishing patch
I'll keep warm
With my neck sunk
Beneath my shoulder blades
I'll wait till the tide turns
And the water recedes
There will be fish
Lingering in the shallows
I know their hiding places

LITTLE BLACKBIRD

In winter
You know where to find the tasty morsels
You toss the fallen leaves
The little creatures scurry
Too late
Your bright yellow beak picks them up
You have been busy from early morning
Scratching in the soil
Along the raised beds
Looking for snails
There is abundance of provision for you
You know where to find it
Near the pot plants
Empty shells lie scattered
When I open the door
You rise and dart over the fence
You will come back to forage later

EMPTY NEST

No popping of the toaster
Or the kettle boiling for tea and coffee
The highchair is empty
Till the next grandchild comes to visit
No airport pickups today
Visitors from faraway places
England, Canada and India have left
The light, warmth and stillness
Invites us outside
The calm after the storm
Our friend the robin welcomes us
He flutters and swirls around me, excited
Others birds in the forest
Sing their hearts out
Two blue tits come down inquisitively
Looking for food
A solitary crow picks titbits

Scattered on the lawn.
The sunshine glistens on the water
Thousands of lights dancing
Tinkle, tinkle, tinkle
Sounds come up from the last yacht
Below in the bay
I look up to the blue sky
A few dry leaves drift past
Beyond the bare branches
Somewhere up there
My son and his family return to Canada
I will not be sad
Didn't we encourage our children
To adventure beyond the parish

TIME TO FLY

Up, in the sky above
Flying to the ones I love
Bright white clouds reflect the light
Warmth from sunlight feels alright

See the aircraft over there
Heading west with trails of air
A jet plane flies up close
Phew, I'm glad it flew under us

Gaps in clouds, I look down,
I see rivers, lakes and towns
Flight attendant comes around
Coffee, tea and treats abound

Sure to sustain and refresh
The early travellers on request

It is quiet now, Only the sound
Of droning engines all around.

Some asleep to rest a while
Others chat, or joke and smile
Last chance to purchase now
Gifts that are sure to whow

Perfume, watches or makeup
Which gift now will you take up
The pilot tells us "It's time to land,"
Better get ready with bags at hand

Won't be long till we are on the ground
Ryanair likes a quick turn around.
Seat belt lights give the sign
No longer needed
We've arrived

SLOVAKIA

Under a willow tree in Slovakia
My body welcomes the warm sun
With the creatures
That had to endure the long winter

Life is breaking forth all around me
Sparrows chirp above me in the branches
Taking turns to fly into crevices in the wall
Building their nests for their young

I survey the green of the forest trees
Two weeks ago they were bare brown
    trunks
Doves call from their midst
The apple trees burst forth buds and flowers

Attracting bees that buzz and hum

Busy collecting nectar and pollen
White butterflies float in the air
Outlined by the green leaves

Although a thousand miles apart
We share familiar wildlife in our gardens
My son Aaron works the soil
Marta is planting flowers

Free from washing dishes and clothes
Cooking, baking, cleaning
The children play nearby
Safe in the space of the new mown lawn

A hose gushes cool water
The boys chase and squeal
Darting in and out of the spray
Barbeque smoke drifts through the air

Inviting us to the picnic table
Grilled chicken, courgettes, pineapple
Sweetcorn and mushrooms are ready
Lets dive in

THE YOUNG HERON

Cars hurry to the ferry
Lovers chat
Strong youths hike along the shore road
Cyclists sprint past
Unaware of the heron
Standing nearby
On the water's edge
Still
Long legs stiff
Dignified
With long, wispy feathers
Dangling from his chest
Slender neck outstretched
Head tilted
Eyes staring
Glaring
Yellow beak darts and stabs

A small fish is swallowed
Rewarded
Satisfied
Savouring success
Rest for a while
Head wound into his shoulders
He waits into the night
Fishing
He knows that tomorrow
There will be choppy waters
He shrieks
Spreads his feathers
Like a skirt hanging from his wings
And rises to the hills beyond
To wait high in a tree
Till the storm passes

THE BUTTERFLY

Oh white butterfly
In Nugent's Wood, Portaferry
You live in my orchard
You surprised me in Toronto
You passed by the rugby match in Etobicoke
You fluttered across the lawn in Mass-
    achusetts
Were you at the Pinnacle in New
    Hampshire?
You rested on the lilac tree in Maine
You spread your wings in Gloucester
You sat on a stone in Newbury Port
You smelt the flowers on Lough Erie shore
You welcomed me in Turin
You flew high in Hamilton
You dance in my garden
To welcome me home

Your wings have grown
You glide effortlessly over the roof
You have brought your family to say hello
They kiss the dandelion and the daisy
You were hiding when it rained
The sunshine has returned
Spread your wings again.

WORM MOON

You appear in the east
A ball of cold fire
Then a white light
As you rise in the sky
Pulling oceans across shores
Calling worms out of soil
Energising seeds to open
Telling farmers when to sow
And when to harvest
Calling the birds to migrate
And navigate their way to new climes
Giving light to the fox and the badger
To find food, while their young play
At the mouth of their dens
Till morning when you go down in the west
And let one brighter arise

THE TURNSTONE

Come stop
Do you hear the click, click, click
Along the shore
A flurry of turnstones
Heads bobbing up and down busily
Their beaks turn over stones
Brown and white feathers
Camouflaged
Against the brown wet seaweed
Glistening in the sun
Looking for insects
Tasty moist morsels
On upturned pebbles
Ignore your phone
Do you see the darting bodies
Do you hear

They are visiting from Greenland
Forget about shopping
Don't worry
Dinner can wait
Come stay a while

THE BLACKTHORN

In April your white flowers
Cover our hedgerows like snow
Solitary bees awaken at your scent
Sweet nectar and pollen to sustain
Your thorns protect the sparrow
As he builds his nest
No animal dares to break out
The farmer's choice for a strong fence
In Autumn I look for your brown fruit
A healing fruit of nutrients
To ward off sickness through the winter
Your branches are cut and straightened
To make a walking stick
Or a weapon to defend
Thorns like yours
Were wound into a crown for a King
And by His stripes we are healed.

BLACKBIRD SINGING IN THE NIGHT

The Christmas lights are bright
In the dead of night
A lone blackbird is singing
Is he announcing good news
Is he calling for attention
Like the multitude of heavenly hosts
Announcing Jesus' birth to the shepherds
Singing Glory to God in the highest
And on earth good will to all men
There is room for me in the inn.
In a soft plush bed
Because He was born in a straw lined
    manger
He became poor
So I could become rich

BECAUSE THE NIGHT, I WRITE

When the night comes
I unwind
I love this quiet time
Everyone asleep
No noise
No television
No one needing my attention
No cooking to be done
During this time
I reflect on the day past
And prepare for the day ahead
I sleep
I awaken in the dark
To read my Bible
For inspiration
Then I write

MORNING GLORY

The full moon is on my right
High in the sky.
The sun is rising to my left
An aeroplane flies south
Just in front of the moon.
It is lit up by the light of the sun
The sky is changing from water colours
Of pink and purple to pale blue
It will get brighter and warmer
A dozen sheep form a line
As they walk down to the meadow opposite
To graze in the warmth of the rising sun
Their thirst will be quenched
From the dew on the grass.
September roses open up again
Swallows twitter, swirl
And rest on the telephone wires

Gathering for their exit to the south
A robin twitters
He is sitting on the fence
He will stay close all winter
He will endure the Irish weather
Sun, wind or cold
The heavens declare the glory of God
The skies proclaim the work of his hands
In the heavens
God has pitched a tent for the sun
It is like a bridegroom
Coming out of his chamber
Like a champion rejoicing to run his course
It rises at one end of the heavens
And follows its course to the other end.[1]

OLD AND GREY

*a*n Arctic Tern was taking sanctuary along the seashore today. It was warm in the morning sunshine and sheltered from the wind in a bend of the shoreline and safe from danger. Normally the terns are in pairs or a group along the shore. This bird did not look as if it had energy to go diving for food. I took a closer look at the lone bird through the binoculars.

The bird's feathers around the mouth look grey instead of the usual black. The beak and legs were a dark red instead of a brighter red. I think this bird may not have much longer to live. It has taken sanctuary in this quiet place to spend its last few days. No more flights around the world for this bird.

I believe other birds retire here to spend their last days. They may have lost a mate or their life span is nearly over. I have noticed different birds that hang out nearby on their own, a black-backed gull, an oystercatcher and a curlew. This coast must be the place where grey haired people like us, and grey feathered creatures come to live. Their life work of rearing young is coming to an end.

> Even when I am old and grey do not forsake
> me my God[1]

PHEASANTS COME TO REST

I am sitting by my bedroom window early taking a few moments to praise and thank God when a movement at the side of the lawn caught my eye. I watched as a mother pheasant followed by five young chicks walked into our garden.

There is dead, brown vegetation as well as green grass there. The five chicks were spread out looking for seeds in the mixture of vegetation on the verge of the lawn. The vigilant mother was on the look out for danger. One chick with feathers like a necklace, ventured further than the others. He must be a young male. His coloured neck feathers were beginning to show.

I enjoyed the scene for some minutes. I want a closer look. I got my binoculars. The hen stops, relaxes and preens her feathers. She stretches her wings, ruffles her feathers and scratches her back feathers. I could see the pattern on her feathers as she picked through them. Her overall colour blended well into the background of brown vegetation. Her chicks investigated the foliage around her. They had no fear while their mum was close by.

A farmer is harvesting his crop of wheat over the fence from where we live. Beyond the field is a forest. Perhaps the pheasant family were disturbed because of the noisy farm machinery. The wheat would be their convenient supply of food.

I imagine that God had supplied a whole field of wheat for this pleasant pheasant family. If God can care for these creatures how much more will He care for me and my family. We are more important than the birds of the air.

What are the main things people worry about: health, lack of money, how to look after their children, what to eat, being alone, where to live?

Have faith in God, who promises if we seek him first he will add all things unto us. I can testify to God's provision for food, houses, and health for my family of fourteen children.

It is true what Jesus said,

> Can any one of you by worrying add a single hour to your life?[1]

CHRISTMAS SEAGULLS

I was looking at the birds today, learning from them. I parked beside the shore on this December morning and watched some gulls having a happy time in the water.

It is high tide, beauty treatment time! The gulls are cleaning, dipping, diving, dashing, dunking, dancing, splashing, stretching, swaying, playing and bathing.

They are free. They circle overhead and come back to base. There isn't a strong, cold wind with which to contend. There are no angry waves dashing against the shore, just gentle ripples flowing. The sun's rays warm them. They are enjoying being together with others of their kind. They are being cared for by their Heavenly Father.

Why do we not learn from the birds particularly at this time of the year. There is too much worrying, shopping, spending, eating, drinking, stressing, rushing, driving and cooking in preparation for Christmas.

I must take time to rest and enjoy my little flock.

> Come to me all you who are weary and
> burdened and I will give you rest. Take
> my yoke upon you and learn from me,
> for I am gentle and humble in heart, and
> you will find rest for your souls. For my
> yoke is easy and my burden light.[1]

SEA BIRDS THIRST FOR WATER

I awoke to the sound of half a dozen Brent Geese down at the water's edge below our home. They came for a drink of fresh water from a stream that enters the sea there.

They wait for each other to drink then the whole group fly off, their outstretched wings, with white V markings on the tail, blend with the colour of the moving water and disappear into the distance.

As I watched the wildlife from my window, I was reminded of the Holy Spirit. I believe God our creator wants us to drink from the flowing river of the Holy Spirit coming from heaven and rest a while, like the geese coming to the stream.

Jesus told the woman at the well he could give her water and she would never thirst again. He said,

Jesus said,

Everyone who drinks this water will be
thirsty again, but whoever drinks the
water I give them will never thirst.
Indeed, the water I give them will
become in them a spring of water welling
up to eternal life. [1]

The Holy Spirit is the living water that Jesus promised.
He is described as the river that flows from the throne of
God. Isaiah invites us to come to the water.

Come, all you who are thirsty, come to the
waters; and you who have no money,
come, buy and eat! Come, buy wine and
milk without money and without cost. [2]

I was certainly thirsty after rearing our children. I was
tired and weary. I needed refreshment. I was healed from
cancer but my mind needed healed from the trauma of
having cancer and the pain of my children leaving home
and other disappointments. I was a good candidate for the
water of life that Jesus talked about.

As I spend time praying in the Holy Spirit I get
refreshed and have new strength. No matter what age we
are, we still run out of strength if we are too busy. We
need life from God to renew our energy. Very often life
makes us weary. But God invites us to come to him to get
a drink of refreshing water to nourish our thirsty souls.

DUNLINS

*W*hen we return from travelling, Brendan and I like to get out into nature. We drove to Newcastle where the Mourne mountains rise from the sea. A few days ago the waves were crashing, splashing, and cascading onto the promenade, leaving sea weed and sand. Now the tide is high and the sea calm, with waves gently lapping on the rocks.

We walked along the promenade. I looked closer at an area of beach covered in pebbles. There was a little flock of Dunlins. Their tiny bodies, white bellies and grey backs camouflaged them among the stones. They were still and silent in unison, all facing the same direction. The moment reminded me when people are silent out of respect for someone important. It looked like they were worshipping. It was a holy moment.

Can we learn from these little birds and be in unity?

Sometimes one can be quiet personally but for a group to stand in quietness is unusual.

Our world is so full of noise and distraction. Perhaps we can learn from the Dunlins.

> God is our refuge and strength, an ever-present help in trouble. Therefore we will not fear, though the earth give way and though its waters roar and foam. Be still, and know that I am God. [1]

THRUSHES IN WINTER

*L*ast week, cold winds brought snow that overwhelmed our homes and roads. Red alert warnings told us to stay at home. A nearby Tesco Extra store was completely sold out of food. Some people made sure they had food to keep them alive during the cold spell.

Birds also need extra food during cold weather. Many feathered friends came to our bird table in the frosty mornings; blackbirds, wagtails, chaffinch and sparrows. I enjoyed watching them as we sat by the Aga eating our own breakfast.

We have a tree in our garden full of red berries. I noticed a flurry of activity around it. I looked closer. A number of song thrushes were busily feeding on the berries. They flew back and forth from the forest nearby. One bird sat on a branch and kept watch. If any other birds come to the tree it drove them away. Some blackbirds tried to get the bounty. A fight broke out till the intruders flew off.

Now the snow has melted and the thrushes remain in the forest. The Tesco shelves will be filled again. The danger has past. Our regular visitor, the robin will sit on a branch in the hedgerow waiting for our door to open. Waiting for Brendan to feed him.

> Look at the birds. They don't plant or
> harvest or store food in barns, for your
> heavenly father feeds them. [1]

A DISPLAY BEFORE NIGHTFALL

*L*ast November crows gathered nearby on the treetops in the local forest. They stayed over the winter. They had fun each evening before settling down for the night. Hundreds flew into the tops of the branches and called and cawed, welcoming one another until a great crowd gathered.

Then they all lift up into the air spontaneously in a murmuration that swayed and swirled in an amazing display. In strong winds they flew up, hunched their wings and tumbled like fearless skydivers. Each evening we looked forward to their free performance.

Some of the crows have adapted to finding food on the seashore. They stay behind while the others go away to search for food in the country. I saw a crow fly up and drop something on the hard road surface. It was a seashell. The crash on the road opened up the shell and produced a juicy meal.

At nesting time the crows build nests of twigs high up in the branches. One such crow with a twig in his beak was sitting on a branch in my garden. I watched to see where he was building his nest, expecting it to fly off in the direction of the nearby forest. He flew in the direction of my chimney. Oh no!

I rushed outside to investigate. The chimney was covered with wire to stop birds entering but this fellow was able to navigate through a hole in the mesh with a twig in its mouth?

I shouted at the crow. I said, My family is now living in this house. You can find a new home in the forest.

I then lit some paper in the fireplace to smoke the bird out. I was too late. His nest has already blocked the chimney. The smoke filled the room. Brendan found some rods for cleaning chimneys. Sticks and twigs came tumbling down. A workman came and put finer wire mesh that a crow couldn't get through on the chimney pot. I wanted my log fire with family and friends instead of noisy trespassing crows.

The Holy Spirit is often referred to as fire and this crow was blocking my fire. Although many difficulties may come I don't want any obstacle stopping the Holy Spirit in my life. I want my fire to burn bright and warm those around me.

> When the day of Pentecost came, they were
> all together in one place. Suddenly a
> sound like the blowing of a violent wind

came from heaven and filled the whole house where they were sitting. They saw what seemed to be tongues of fire that separated and came to rest on each of them. All of them were filled with the Holy Spirit and began to speak in other tongues as the Spirit enabled them.[1]

Do not put out the fire of the Holy Spirit. Do not treat prophecies with contempt[2]

THE CORMORANT

$\mathcal{I}$ awoke to a warm, bright morning and decided to go for a cycle. My body was telling me it needed some exercise. I felt a bit stiff after sitting at a desk for hours on end. I needed to get away from my computer and books and do some exercise. I needed to get outdoors to see life around me. I prefer cycling to walking. I enjoy pushing my bike along the Loughshore Road.

I noticed a group of birds resting on a small island in the distance. One was flapping its wings, stretching after feeding. It continued to flap and stretch its wings in the sunshine for fifteen minutes. I imagined this cormorant was praising the Lord. Let everything that has breath praise the Lord.

The cormorant keeps his distance from people. On the ferry I often see a lone cormorant as it surfaces after diving for food. Its short legs and streamlined body help him easily glide into the water. Cormorants have been likened to penguins.

Bird Island off Kircubbin is a safe place where cormorants can nest and rear their young. At dusk small groups of them fly low over Strangford Lough on their way back to Bird island.

I thought of the following scripture,

> Praise the Lord from the earth, you great sea
> creatures and all ocean depths, lightning
> and hail, snow and clouds, stormy winds
> that do his bidding, you mountains and
> all hills, fruit trees and all cedars, wild
> animals and all cattle, small creatures and
> flying birds, kings of the earth and all
> nations, you princes and all rulers on
> earth, young men and women, old men
> and children.[1]

HOME FOR CHRISTMAS

I tell my children who are returning for Christmas to make sure they bring warm hats and gloves for I'm planning to go Bird Watching instead of Christmas shopping. I have plenty of binoculars to share and I am blessed to live beside Strangford Lough where many birds come to live. I will not have to organise a long journey. There is a variety of bird life nearby.

It will not cost us money. There will be no temptation to overspend or visit coffee shops. Just a warm flask and a few nibbles will help us to endure. I hope they enjoy it. This will be a change from work and study. Time to breathe fresh air, slow down and hang out together like the birds. Time to heal and be restored. A time for peace.

I am restored in my mind and body as I take time beside still waters. He leads me beside still waters to restore my soul. [1]

I provide a big warm breakfast. Then wrapped up well

with hats, scarves and coats we head down the lane. On our walk beside the lough we see the usual residents, Brent geese, black backed gulls, heron and oystercatchers. Each of the many herons have their own territory.

We hear the sound of stones hitting one another and stop to investigate. We counted ten turnstones, tiny seabirds, busily upturning small stones and feeding on the juicy morsels of insects exposed. The birds were well camouflaged against the brown and grey seaweed and stones. One wouldn't know they were there except for the noise they are making.

On the way home I notice teal ducks who had come ashore to drink fresh water from a nearby brook that trickles into the sea. They were resting and preening their feathers, warming themselves in the morning sunshine. A family of ducks nest in the marshy land just below our house. They raise their young and take them fishing on the shore nearby.

We enjoyed birdwatching together.

THE REDSHANK

oday, over the Christmas season, I went bird watching on my own. I didn't dare disturb my own little flock who were fast asleep.

I saw a wading bird with orange legs and beak and speckled brown body. It is a Redshank that bobs its head, looking here and there as it scans the water's edge. It feeds on insects and molluscs in the mud. When disturbed, it flies up in the air and makes a loud screeching sound.

There is a distinctive "v" shape on its back feathers while in flight. When I checked my bird book I discovered many Redshanks come to winter in Ireland from Iceland.

Iceland is an island north of Ireland on the Arctic Circle. In 2010 a volcano erupted in Iceland spouting ash into the air for days on end. I was suffering from cancer when that volcano erupted.

On my first visit to Iceland I read Psalm 18.

> The ropes of death entangled me. In my
> distress I cried to the Lord. My cry
> reached his ears. Then the earth quaked
> and trembled, The foundations of the
> mountain shook. He rained down hail
> and burning coals. The Lord thundered
> from heaven He reached down from
> heaven and rescued me.[1]

I believe God heard my cry and healed me from cancer. He rescued me from death. Through this scripture I believe God showed me what he did for me. The all powerful God who opens the mountains and lets fire flow out, healed me.

He was angry that I was dying from cancer. He touched me to show His power to heal. He wants people to know that He heals and He wants me to make it known. God reminding me what He did for me when I found that Redshank from Iceland along the lough shore.

A SPARROW FALLS TO THE GROUND

When Brendan and I traveled with our family on holiday down through Ireland, we realised there was plenty of empty space in the countryside. When we flew over Canada and other nations we saw thousands of miles of wide open space below. Even Slovakia was full of wide open fields, valleys and plenty of uninhabited land. Brendan often says, The world is practically empty. God didn't create a a small overcrowded world

I agree with Brendan. Why do people say there is not enough room on the earth for people to live? Why do people want to control the population of the world, saying there is not enough food? Will not God look after mankind, whom he made in his image.

In these open places wildlife abound. No one sees this abundance of life except God. We have the privilege of admiring the wild life that turns up near where we live.

The blackbirds in our garden, the fox that comes to steal our chickens, or the swallows and the swans that fly overhead. Where do they lay their head at night?

Jesus said,

> "Foxes have dens and birds have nests, but
> the Son of Man has no place to lay his
> head."1

The majority of people today only get a glimpse of the beauty of living creatures from nature programmes. In Job the writer says,

> "Where were you when I laid the earth's
> foundation? Tell me, if you understand.
> Have you journeyed to the springs of the sea
> or walked in the recesses of the deep?
> Have you comprehended the vast expanses
> of the earth? Tell me, if you know all this.
> Who gives the ibis wisdom or gives the
> rooster understanding?
> "Do you hunt the prey for the lioness and
> satisfy the hunger of the lions?
> Who provides food for the raven when its
> young cry out to God and wander about
> for lack of food?
> "Do you know when the mountain goats
> give birth? Do you watch when the doe
> bears her fawn?

Their young thrive and grow strong in the
wilds; they leave and do not return. "Who
let the wild donkey go free? Who untied
its ropes? I gave it the wasteland as its
home, the salt flats as its habitat.
"Will the wild ox consent to serve you? Will
it stay by your manger at night?[1]

We only ever see a small part of what God has created.
He cares for it all. I saw a dead sparrow today. It reminded
me of the verse when Jesus said,

Are not two sparrows sold for a penny? Yet
not one of them will fall to the ground
outside your Father's care. So don't be
afraid; you are worth more than many
sparrows.[2]

LAST WALK BEFORE LEAVING

I love to walk along the Loughshore Road in Portaferry in the mornings. I often see the regular visitors. All kinds of birds, ducks, geese, swans, sea gulls, oystercatchers, and waders are feeding, swimming or resting.

One morning a flock of birds were circling around. I had not seen them before. I checked my bird book. There on the front cover was my new discovery, a bird with a few feathers sticking up from its crown, a Lapwing.

The Lapwing has green feathers on his back and wings. His underbody is white. They gather in flocks. Their black under feathers make up a full wing span and aides it to spin, twist and dive in flight. This bird is distinctive because of the tuft of feathers on his head.

The day before we left Portaferry I took a walk by myself to reflect on the changes up ahead and say farewell to the birds that have been my neighbours for six years.

A group of lapwings came to visit. They were resting on a stretch of rock cut off by the tide. They were within easy sight as the full tide allowed the water to separate them from danger. I could see their dark green back feathers and their tufts of head feathers.

As I approached one bird took flight and the whole group flew off. I stopped to look and followed their flight. They turned, swirled and circled up and up in the sky above me till they were out of sight.

I continued on towards home, happy. I was feeling comforted and delighted to have caught the display of the lapwings. It seemed like they put on a final show for me, saying farewell. I'm leaving Ballyhenry House to move to Belfast. I will miss Portaferry so much. But our children and grandchildren want us to live near them.

Today I read from Revelation about winged creatures in heaven, worshiping God continually.

> Each of these living beings had six wings,
>   and their wings were covered all over
>   with eyes, inside and out. Day after day
>   and night after night they keep on saying,
> "Holy, holy, holy is the Lord God, the
>   Almighty, the one who always was, who
>   is, and who is still to come." You are
>   worthy, O Lord our God, to receive glory
>   and honour and power. For you created
>   everything, And it is for your pleasure
>   that they exist and were created. [1]

WALKING THE DOG

*O*ur big Scottish deerhound called Finn needed regular walks. Most Saturday mornings Brendan took us all for a drive. Often we'd go to the beach. When he heard the minibus start Finn came bouncing through the garden, jumped into our yellow minibus and started licking the children.

One morning we went to Tyrella beach. The fresh sea air cleared our sleepy heads. Our boys and girls spread out over the sandy space. Finn leapt and bounded from Brendan and me to the children and back again. It wss wonderful to watch him stretch his long legs and race up the shore. Freedom in motion.

At the end of the beach hundreds of sea birds were gathered beside a freshwater stream in the morning sun. Finn sped towards them and the entire flock exploded high into the warm morning air. It's great to see Finn and our children full of life, running, laughing and chasing one another. We walked and talked together. The older children looked out for the younger ones holding hands or carrying a tired one on the shoulder.

Brendan gave a loud whistle and we all returned slowly to the minibus. Finn was the last to jump aboard. He vigorously shook himself and sprayed us all with seawater. Jesus said,

> "You are the salt of the earth. But if the salt
> loses its saltiness, how can it be made
> salty again? It is no longer good for
> anything, except to be thrown out and
> trampled underfoot. [1]

Brendan had to make many sacrifices in order to move to new homes with his family. When we moved from Downpatrick to Bright our new landlord did not allow pets. Reluctantly Brendan had to part with his beloved dog Finn. Ruth and Stuart agreed to look after him in Scotland.

When we lived in Coleraine Brendan had an Irish Wolfhound called *Shadow*. Everyone knew our big dog. She was part of the family. So much so, when Brendan wanted to breed her she was not interested in another dog.

It was difficult for Brendan when we moved from Coleraine. We couldn't take *Shadow* with us. She went to live with our daughter Shann who lived in the country. Brendan went for one last walk along the River Bann with

Shadow. Just then sixteen swans made loud honking sounds as they flew low overhead. They were flying south for the winter just like Brendan and me and our fourteen children.

BEAUTIFUL BELFAST

*a*fter six wonderful years in Ballyhenry House, Portaferry, it was time to move on. My healing was complete and like the Brent Geese we needed to be in other places. Covid lockdowns were still in place and our children wanted us nearer them in Belfast. We moved to Haypark Avenue just off the Ormeau Road. Our children Nora and Ruth and their husbands helped us pack and move. Downsizing was awful. Although in my heart I knew it was time to move I still often felt paralysed.

A ministry friend called Lionel Batke visited in October. He kept singing an old pentecostal song called *Moving Forward for God.* Little did we think we would be moving so soon after Lionel traveled home to Canada. Another lady visited us as we were packing up our stuff. She prophesied I would meet a female neighbour in Belfast who would be a blessing to me.

Brendan found the move difficult. He missed nature

and the sea views. We moved during the lockdown. We were all confined to our homes, except for walks.

One morning I heard a neighbour power washing our back alley. From a grimy grey passageway she restored it to a fresh white cemented alleyway. Brendan and I added many of our plant pots. Others in our neighbourhood have developed their outdoor space. We now gather in the sunshine for a chat or rest in the evening sunshine.

Café Nero is at the end of our street. I often go there for coffee with friends. Four of our children live nearby.

Although he believed it was God's will for us to come to Belfast, Brendan was still struggling with the smaller house. He was missing nature, which he calls, *God's First Bible*.

One day he looked at me and said, Angela I need some reassurance that we'd done the right thing.

That night I awoke and went up to my new office and picked down one of the dozens of book I have journaled in. I opened the jotter to a page where I had written the word Haypark. The page was dated 2015.

Next morning over breakfast I produced the old jotter and showed Brendan the page. I had written,

- Luke 10 – Authority to heal.
- Jesus has conquered.
- Church, Church, Church.
- Haypark.
- Connections.
- On a mission.

- We have fought wars.
- Stretch, stretch.

In Luke 10, Jesus told His disciples the harvest was plentiful, but the workers were few. He then sent them out, two by two, like lambs among wolves. He said,

> When you enter a house, first say, 'Peace to
> this house.' If someone who promotes
> peace is there, your peace will rest on
> them; if not, it will return to you. Stay
> there, eating and drinking whatever they
> give you, for the worker deserves his
> wages. Do not move around from house
> to house. When you enter a town and are
> welcomed, eat what is offered to you.
> Heal the sick who are there and tell them,
> 'The kingdom of God has come near to
> you . . . Whoever listens to you listens to
> me; whoever rejects you rejects me; but
> whoever rejects me rejects him who sent
> me.'

Luke 10 also says,

> The seventy-two returned with joy and said,
> "Lord, even the demons submit to us in
> your name." Jesus replied, "I saw Satan
> fall like lightning from heaven. I have

given you authority to trample on snakes and scorpions and to overcome all the power of the enemy; nothing will harm you. However, do not rejoice that the spirits submit to you, but rejoice that your names are written in heaven."

Brendan and I realised this six year old piece of writing was telling us God had sent us to Belfast on a mission and had given us the authority to heal the sick and cast out demons. There would be connections with people and churches and we would be stretched in the process. But the word that encouraged Brendan the most was the word Haypark for we were now living in Haypark Avenue, Belfast.

When Brendan asked me why I had written the word Haypark I had to admit I had no idea. In fact I'd no memory whatsoever of writing anything on this page and I'd never ever knowingly heard of Haypark Avenue.

Yet God had answered Brendan's prayer and I was encouraged. God knew we'd be living in Haypark and He told me this one night six years earlier. My constant desire is to hear God's voice and do God's will. I always want to be available for God and to be in the right place at the right time doing God's will in the right way.

Yet change is rarely easy. There's always the temptation to be like the children of Israel who when God moved them on, moaned and longed for the past. They said,

In Egypt we sat around pots filled with meat
and ate all the bread we wanted. But
now you have brought us into this
wilderness to starve us to death.[1]

Brendan and I believe it is better to be like

Abraham who, by faith, when called to go to
a place he would later receive as his
inheritance, obeyed and went, without
knowing where he was going. By faith he
dwelt in the promised land as a stranger
in a foreign country. He lived in tents, as
did Isaac and Jacob, who were heirs with
him of the same promise. For he was
looking forward to the city with founda-
tions, whose architect and builder is
God.[2]

God brought us to Portaferrry for six years and
blessed us. The same God has brought us to Haypark
Avenue for His purposes and He will bless us here as well.

NOTES

2. INTRODUCTION

1. Proverbs 13:12
2. Matt 6:25-35
3. Isaiah 30:26

3. RESTORATION

1. Jeremiah 33:6 The Message
2. Numbers 26:50

4. LOOK FOR THE ANCIENT PATHWAYS

1. Matt 5:9
2. Psalm 133:1 NIV
3. Jer 6:16 NLT

5. AFTER CANCER

1. Proverbs 14 v 4

6. THE BLACKBIRD MAKES HIS NEST

1. Matt 18:20
2. Psalm 84:3 NLT

8. EVERY MAN NEATH HIS VINE AND FIG TREE

1. 1 Kings 4:25 NLT
2. Micah 4;4 KJV

9. THE FERRYMEN

1. Psalm 121

10. SPRING VISITORS

1. John 10:10 NLT
2. Song of Solomon 2:12 NLT

11. GUILLEMOTS

1. Isaiah 61:6

12. THE PRINCESS CUP

1. Psalm 20 v 4

13. BEAUTIFUL MOSAICS

1. Isaiah 64:8
2. 1 Peter 4:12

14. A FARMER PLOUGHING

1. Mark 4 v 26
2. Isaiah 61 v 11

15. THE BRENT GEESE

1. Isaiah 40:11 NIV
2. Jer 8:7 NLT

16. TRAVELLING TO THE NATIONS

1. Isaiah 49 v 12
2. Psalm 147 v 3

17. MY BIRTHDAY

1. Isaiah 53:5 NIV

18. BIRD WATCHING FROM MY KITCHEN WINDOW

1. Psalm 34 13:14
2. Isaiah 58:11
3. Psalm 133 v 1/3

19. SWALLOWS ARRIVE FROM AFRICA

1. Jeremiah 8 v 7

21. THE TERNS HAVE ARRIVED

1. Gen 1 v 20

22. EAGLES IN CANADA

1. Isaiah 40 v 31

23. SWANS

1. Proverbs 22 v 6

25. THE CHAFFINCH

1. Isaiah 53: 3-5

POEMS

1. Psalm 45:1

38. MORNING GLORY

1. Psalm 19:4/6

39. OLD AND GREY

1. Psalm 71 v 18

40. PHEASANTS COME TO REST

1. Matt 6 v 27

41. CHRISTMAS SEAGULLS

1. Matt 11 v 28

42. SEA BIRDS THIRST FOR WATER

1. John 4 v 10
2. Isaiah 55 v 1, 3

43. DUNLINS

1. Psalm 46 v 10

44. THRUSHES IN WINTER

1. Matt 6:25-34

45. A DISPLAY BEFORE NIGHTFALL

1. Acts 2 v 1-4
2. 1 These 5 v 19-20

46. THE CORMORANT

1. Psalm 148 v 7

47. HOME FOR CHRISTMAS

1. Psalm 23 v 3

48. THE REDSHANK

1. Psalm 18 v 4

49. A SPARROW FALLS TO THE GROUND

1. Job
2. Matt 10:29

50. LAST WALK BEFORE LEAVING

1. Rev 4 v 11

51. WALKING THE DOG

1. Matthew 5:13

52. BEAUTIFUL BELFAST

1. Exodus 16:3
2. Hebrews 11:8-10

Printed in Great Britain
by Amazon

23604271R00086